P is for PURPOSE

Alphabet Affirmations

Written by: J. Lavone Roberson

Illustrated by: Senetha Fuller

Dedication

To God. Thank you.
I dedicate this book to Jon'Aja Beamon ... my Jay-Jay. You are AMAZING. You are BEAUTIFUL. You are BLESSED. You are WORTHY. God made you perfectly. I love you forever and always. I pray you always see yourself as God and I see you. I am so proud of you.

Copyright

Library of Congress: 2021917393
ISBN: 978-1-7365371-8-3 (Paperback)
Also Available as an E-Book
Printed in USA.
10 9 8 7 6 5 4 3 1
Second Edition
September 2021

AFFIRMATION

af-firm-a-tion
noun

1. A word of phrase repeated to oneself to declare a certain feeling or belief.

2. The declaration that something is true.

3. The act of manifesting a mindset and becoming the person or thing you wish to be or that you are.

"It's the repetition of affirmations that leads to belief. And once that belief becomes a deep conviction, things begin to happen."
-Muhammed Ali

Social Emotional Learning:

5 Ways to improve a child's self-esteem:

1. **Be consistent.** Consistency and routines help to build trust.
2. **Ask their input.** Children know very early on how they feel, what they like, and what they dislike.
3. **Allow them to help** and reward their efforts with positive praise.
4. **Compliment them and affirm them.** Let them know how AMAZING they are and how proud you are of them.
5. **Create new experiences together.** Field trips, adventures, crafts, cooking together, etc… are great ways to bond and create memories as a family.

I am AMAZING.

I am APPRECIATIVE.

I am AWESOME.

I am AMBITIOUS.

I am ALIVE.

I am ADORED.

I am ARTISTIC.

Cc

I am COURAGEOUS.

I am CARING.

I am CAREFUL.

I am COOL.

I am CREATIVE.

I am CONFIDENT.

C is for cuddling!

Dd

I am DIFFERENT.

I am DARING.

I am DYNAMIC.

I am DIVINE.

I am DELIGHTFUL.

Ee

I am EVOLVING.

I am EQUAL.

I am ENOUGH.

I am EMPOWERED.

I am EXCITED.

I am ENTHUSIASTIC.

I am ENLIGHTENED.

I am EMPOWERED.

Ff

I am FREE.

I am FUN.

I am FRIENDLY.

I am FOCUSED.

F is for fishing!

Ii

I am INTELLIGENT.
I am INCLUSIVE.
I am INSPIRING.

Jj

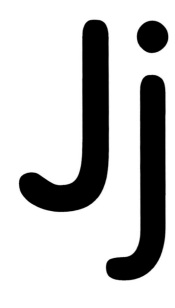

I am JOYFUL.

I am a JOKING.
I am JOLLY.

Kk

I am KIND.
I am KNOWLEDGEABLE.

Ll

I am LOVED.
I am LOVEABLE.
I am LOVING.
I am LOVE.
I am LOYAL.
I am LEARNING.
I am LISTENING.
I am LIVING.

Mm

I am MAGICAL.
I am MOTIVATED.
I am MIRACULOUS.
I am MAGNIFICENT.
I am ME.

Nn

I am NICE.
I am NOBLE.
I am NOTICED.
I am NOTORIOUS.

Oo

I am OUTSTANDING.
I am OPTIMISTIC.
I am OKAY.

Pp

I am PATIENT.
I am POSITIVE.
I am PASSIONATE.
I am PEACEFUL.

I am PLAYFUL.
I am PRECIOUS.
I am POWERFUL.
I am PROUD.

My name is Nia, Nia means purpose.

I have PURPOSE.

Scan for more info.

I am QUIET.
I am QUALITY.
I am QUALIFIED.

Rr

I am ROYALTY.
I am RESPECTFUL.
I am RESOURCEFUL.
I am RADIANT.
I am READY.
I am RECEPTIVE.
I am RELAXED.
I am REFRESHED.
I am RELIEVED.
I am RENEWED.
I am RESILIENT.

Ss

I am SAFE.
I am SMART.
I am SILLY.
I am SPECIAL.
I am SINCERE.
I am SUCCESSFUL.
I am STRONG.
I am SPECTACULAR.
I am SENSATIONAL.

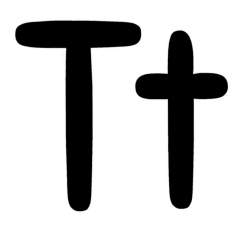

Tt

I am TERRIFIC.
I am TRYING.
I am TALENTED.
I am TRUSTWORTHY.
I am THANKFUL.

Uu

I am UNIQUE.
I am UNDERSTANDING.
I am UPLIFTING.
I am UNLIMITED.

Vv

I am VICTORIOUS.
I am VALUABLE.
I am VIBRANT.

Ww

I am WISE.
I am WORTHY.
I am WINNING.
I am WHOLE.
I am WONDERFUL.

Xx

I am eXtraordinary!

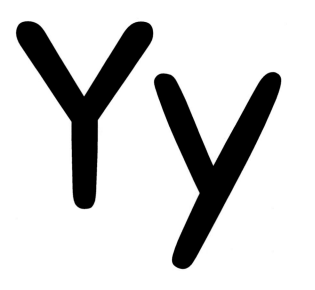

Yy

I am YOUTHFUL.

Zz

I am ZESTY.
I am Zen.
I am ZANY.

Affirmation Activities

1. Add your own affirmations on the letter page it goes with.
2. Create your own daily affirmation list. Which words stick out to you.

Example:

- I am BLESSED.
- I am EVOLVING.
- I am HEALTHY.
- I am JOYFUL.
- I am SAFE.

Meet The Author & Illustrator

Jacquelyn "Lavone" Roberson is an author, educator, and philanthropist from Connecticut. Lavone is the CEO and Founder of The Now I Am Nia Foundation, Inc., where she leads various projects to support communities in need. Lavone is an alumni of Hampton University and a member of Delta Sigma Theta Sorority, Incorporated. She has a B.S. in Sociology, a Master's in Elementary Education,

and an ABD Doctorate in Educational Leadership. As a teacher she was selected to be in the nation's first Quad-D lab classroom cohort. When she is not teaching or working in the community, she enjoys spending time with her family, god children, and MaltiPoo Worthy. To learn more please visit www.NowIAmNia.org and follow us @NowIAmNiaBooks. 1 Corinthians 10:31

Senetha Fuller resides in Philadelphia, PA. She specializes in "urban art" but can create custom art using different mediums. It has always been her passion to inspire through her art. @Red_Panda_Artz

Made in the USA
Columbia, SC
21 December 2021

51443792R00020